MW01226800

Our goal is to help you fall in love with yourself,
in whatever way is needed. We encourage a
Mind, Body and Soul approach.
This is our Blueprint. We hope it helps you
build the best version of yourself.

-Phyl, Allan, Tory, Kris & Desy (the staff)

@Alternative Aging & Medispa

Mind:

The way we talk to ourselves is incredibly important; it affects our mood, our self-image and our hopes for the future. The most important step in learning to love yourself *is giving yourself the chance to do so*. Basically, your brain needs you to practice grace. Start by making the decision that change is possible –then give yourself the grace to learn a new way of thinking.

Letting go of the Old: As a survival mechanism, we tend to remember, and ruminate, over the negative things people have said to us. We are equally inclined to mentally replay instances where we felt embarrassed or made big mistakes. This is totally natural and EVERYONE does it. Everyone. For me personally, the trick to overcoming these thoughts was telling myself that no one else remembers them – or cares to remember them. Which is the truth. How often do you think about other people's short-comings? And unless we are talking about your partner (more on that later) I'm guessing the answer is – not very often. We are immensely preoccupied with ourselves. Realizing that no one else cares or remembers those occasional social mishaps is incredibly freeing. If no one else cares- why should you? You naturally give others grace, and others naturally give you grace. We are all human. No one is perfect. And absolutely no one else cares about that stupid thing you said in fifth grade. Deep breath. Let it go.

Making the "New" easier:

Pay attention to your internal dialogue: Tell yourself good things about yourself. Change that "I'm so clumsy" to "I'm the most graceful person ever", ...or better yet "I'm a ninja." Make it okay to laugh at yourself. Just use positive language when you do, and it won't take long for your confidence to improve.

Don't participate in the double negatives: Our brains don't recognize the word "not" when we process information. Don't use "That's not bad", instead say "That turned out great." Give yourself credit where credit is due.

Watch where you put your energy: This one is life-changing. Think about how much energy (time, emotion, effort, nagging – they all require energy) you expend on things you have absolutely no control over. Then step back and decide if those things really deserve your energy. They don't. Really. Don't put your energy there.

Start Meditation (AKA Mindfulness): This can be super difficult and feel really weird the first couple of times. But, it is SO GOOD for us. Especially those of us that are neurodivergent (ADD, ADHD, Autism, etc.) Look for the Step-by-Step Guide for Meditation Newbies in the **Soul** section.

Big Brain Work:

Take care of your brain. Get counseling. Trauma is a real-life thing. You deserve to heal.

YOU DESERVE TO HEAL.

You deserve happiness.

If this is hard to hear, or makes you feel uncomfortable – this message is meant exactly for you.

Getting there isn't easy. It takes work. It takes intention. It takes letting go of habits, and people, and beliefs. And it takes a whole lot of forgiveness.

Don't fool yourself – you need help for this kind of healing. Find a counselor you like, that you can open up to, but that challenges you too – remember, we are putting in the work here, we want long-term happiness. Even if that means sitting with some hard emotions to get there. We are including some links in the Resources section to get you started on your journey to finding a counselor that works for you.

Body:

You only get one body – take care of it. Our goal here at Alternative Aging & Medispa is to help you do that in the healthiest way possible.

Get in the right mind-set:

Let's start with a little self-reflection. Literally.

Go to your bathroom. Strip down to your under clothes (or *get naked* – that's even better). Look in the mirror. Really look at you. You are beautiful. Your body has gotten you through so many things. It has carried all your troubles, all your hardships. It has been exhausted and neglected and sleep deprived. It has fought hard for you to survive. Look at your body. Run your hands over all the bumps and curves and sore spots. And look in the mirror and tell your body that you see it. Tell it that you love it, and are thankful for getting you this far. And then tell it that from now on – you will appreciate it, and take care of it to the best of your ability. And promise yourself that you will work toward change – not because you "hate" certain parts of yourself, but because your body deserves to be taken care of. It deserves to be loved.

Our Bodies Need Food (and water... so much water):

Hydration: Drink plenty of water. A good rule of thumb – you need half your body weight in ounces. For example, if you weigh 150 pounds, you should be drinking about 75 ounces of water daily (about 5 bottles). Being well hydrated enables the entire body to work better, easier. Including making the fat dissolving process more efficient. So, if your goal is fat loss – drink, drink, drink.

Food: Don't try to change your eating habits overnight – that never lasts long term. Instead, add nutritious snacks. Eat all the colors! Fill your day, and plate, with fruits and veggies. When you start feeding your body the things it needs, it stops craving the fake substitutes.

Our Bodies Need Exercise (a body in motion, stays in motion):

There are no miracle treatments (although, in my opinion, the EMSCULPTneo is pretty close). If you want to be fit & healthy – you need to MOVE YOUR BODY. Even the gentlest exercises - walking, swimming, yoga – are immensely beneficial. Aim for small changes in your daily routine; take the stairs, park on the far side of the parking lot, spend 5 minutes doing gentle stretches in the morning. Easy to do, easy not to do... the choice is yours. But we made a promise to our bodies, remember? So, get up. You got this.

Our Bodies Need Rest:

Regardless of what time of day you sleep, you should aim for 8 hours of restful sleep daily. Our bodies do a lot of detoxing and fat removal while we sleep. Plus, it's good for our mental well-being.

Soul: (This is where things get fun.)

#EMOTIONAL*asshole*

The goal here is to embrace where you are at. It's okay to know what you want. It's okay to know your worth (and you ARE worth it). It's okay to set boundaries and hold to them; and to walk away from people that drain your energy. It's okay to pursue the things that bring you joy. Embrace all of those emotions. None of them are wrong. You are allowed to feel your feelings, while also handling your... things. Emotion doesn't negate the validity of your stance. You aren't Too Much. You deserve the right to be you, and to be loved as you are.

Be Intentional with Your Time:

Figure out what you enjoy and pursue it. If that means dancing like no one is watching – do it. If that means vegging out on the couch with your bestie, watching Grey's Anatomy reruns – do it. If that means sitting and taking in the sunset, or kickboxing, or crocheting, or painting, or curling up with a book – DO IT. You only get this one life. You can't spend it always waiting for a future where you'll have time – your time is happening now. Be intentional with it – figure out what makes you happy, and do it. Enjoy your life – whatever that looks like for you.

You Only Need ONE:

"How bold one gets when one is sure of being loved,"

-Sigmund Freud, 1882.

Studies have found that you only need ONE adult in your life that truly supports and encourages you – for optimal mental health. This is where picking your partner is HUGE. Develop your self-awareness – figure out what you need from a partner and ask for it. Just ask. None of us can read minds- take the guess work out of it. Then return the favor and ask what they need. (Try not to feel criticized by their needs – try not to think of them as a statement of deficit on your part... we just need what we need.) Having a partner that is willing to learn how to support you, and reciprocating that support, will allow you to be free. How bold we become when sure of being loved.

*this person does not have to be a spouse – it can be anyone. *Any* adult that is willing to love and support you. You just need ONE.

**also, how powerful is this for kids – one adult. Think how much of an impact we could make by being someone's ONE.

Step-by-Step Guide for Meditation Newbies

(This method is ADD friendly ...in my ADD opinion.)

1. Start by setting a timer for 5 minutes
2. Sit in a comfortable position
3. Close your eyes
4. Notice the sounds around you, pick them out, recognize them, and then dismiss them
5. Notice your body – starting at your toes and working your way up. Notice any aches or pains, acknowledge them – and then move on.
6. Then focus on your breathing – slow inhalation through your nose for a 6 count, then slow exhale through your mouth for a 6 count. Try to get 10.
7. Then allow your mind to do what it wants – instead of trying to "clear your mind" allow the thoughts to come – recognize them as thoughts – and then dismiss them. The best description of this I have heard is – visualize putting the thought on a post-it, and then set it aside, opening space for the next thought to wander in.
8. Do this until your time is up. Then take a moment and appreciate the work you are putting in here – easy to do, easy not to do. Give yourself credit where credit is due.

Notes:

Our Services & Programs

Health & Wellness

Weight Management Program

We use our PUMP (Personalized Upgrade Master Plan) to design goal-specific treatment plans. Our program includes nutritional supplements and counseling, monthly weigh-ins and body scanning, medication management using Semaglutide, and an open invitation to our Yoga sessions.

IV Hydration Therapy

We offer a variety of IV "cocktails" to chose from. Everything from Immunity Boosts to Hang-Over Recovery. Ask us about our IV Menu for more information.

Hormone Replacement Therapy

We have partnered with BioTE and our 503B pharmacy to provide our patients with personalized hormone replacement that is consistent and reliable. We offer lab testing and individualized hormone replacement plans for both men and women.

Energy & Wellness

Enjoy one of our refreshing Energizing Teas while you get your treatments! Or take them to-go for all-day energy. We also offer delicious Protein Shakes (in meal replacement or snack sizes), Protein Iced Coffee, Hot Coffee and Hot Tea. Check out our "Special-Tea" menu for pre-work out and Mom-centered options.

Anti-Aging

EMFace

The latest technology in anti-aging, the EMFace offers a non-surgical, no-needle Face Lift. Erase the years painlessly with four weekly, 20-minute treatments. The results are *stunning*.

Daxxify/Botox

Our personalized neurotoxin treatment plans are developed after a comprehensive evaluation by our Master Injector. We aim for treatments that enhance your features, giving you a naturally refreshed look.

Dermal Fillers

At Alternative Aging & Medispa your wellbeing is our top-priority. We use the RHA collection of fillers for all our filler treatments. This line has been in use in Europe for over 20 years, boasting the best safety and least side effects compared to any other dermal filler on the market. Its patented HA molecule allows for shape and movement that is natural yet long-lasting.

Neora Skin Care

Clean Ingredients. Real Results. We use Neora in every aspect of our Anti-Aging treatments; from EMFace after-care, to Chemical Peel recovery. Neora's Non-GMO, Gluten Free products have a Clean Formula Guarantee, and are suitable for all skin types.

Chemical Peels

During the winter months, take advantage of our 3-Peel Packages to rejuvenate your skin. We use PCA peels in combination with Neora Skin Care products to correct sunspots, and improve texture and tone.

Body

EMSELLA

Our non-invasive, painless, keep-your-clothes-on treatment for pelvic floor health in both men and women. The EMSELLA is FDA approved for the treatment of urinary incontinence... but that's not why it's our favorite ☺

EMSCULPTneo

Less Fat, More Muscle. The EMSCULPTneo can treat 9 body areas – stimulating muscle and burning fat to help you feel stronger, move better, and look tighter. We love that this machine is actually making you healthier. The bonus is feeling better in your clothes.

Yoga

We offer free Yoga Monday-Friday at 1pm. Join us in-house (we have extra mats) or follow along on IG live. We are NOT yoga instructors – we offer a no-judgement, no-pressure, whole body program that is designed for real-life people. Our sessions typically last 15-20 minutes, and recordings are posted on IG so you can participate any time of day.

Referral Program

Send a referral and earn Shop Points! (Up to 5 points per referral!)

Redeem Points In-House:

5 Points

1 EMSELLA treatment, 25 units of Botox,
OR $250 OFF any one syringe of filler

10 Points

1 Neo maintenance treatment, Botox Look of 3
Treatment, $500 OFF any one syringe of filler

15 Points

$750 OFF any EMSCULPTneo OR EMFACE package, 50%
OFF EMSELLA package, 1 FREE syringe of Filler, OR Bank
your Botox: 75 units

30 Points

EMSELLA 6 treatment package

70 Points

EMSCULPTneo: 6 treatment package to any one body area
of choice

80 Points

EMFace: 4 treatment package

Resources:

...because we don't know what we don't know.

Books:

The Slight Edge, by Jeff Olsen.

   (A good book for starting to make changes)

Mindset, by Carol S. Dweck, Ph.D.

   (Identifying your learning habits and thought patterns)

How to Heal Your Metabolism, by Kate Deering.

   (an easy-to-read explanation of how our bodies use food as fuel)

The Body Keeps the Score, by Bessel Van Der Kolk, M.D.

   (...if the Big Brain Work section hit a nerve, this one is for you)

Law of Attraction Planner, available at FreedomMastery.com

   (This is the best planner ever. Plus, it offers good-vibe tips.)

The Relationship Cure, by John M. Gottman, Ph. D. & Joan DeClaire

   (Teaches you how to connect, or reconnect, with your partner.)

Podcasts:

ADHD for Smart Ass Women, Tracy Otsuka

   (start with episode 19 or 100, and skip the Intro)

Online Resources:

DoneFirst.com

   (online diagnosis and medication management of ADHD)

Thriveworks.com

   (Counseling! Use their phone line to set up your account – it's easier, and a real-life person will help you find a counselor that can best meet your needs. Plus, they take insurance.)

TikTok

   (Okay, hear me out. This platform offers insights into many mental health issues; from both professional and personal experiences. Use it. Knowledge is power. And, you aren't alone.)

A Few Thoughts About Food:

Food is the most widely abused anti-anxiety drug, and exercise is the most underutilized antidepressant:

- Separate your emotions from your food. Make meal and snack choices that make your **body** feel better, not your head. (Because, really, you always end up feeling guilty or bad about yourself later. That mental "relief" is only temporary anyway.)
- Having a moment? Do 10 push-ups. Or 10 Squats. Or both. Give your body the dopamine hit it's looking for – **move your body.**

Eat it because you want it – not because it's there.

- We often underestimate the amount of food we eat, because we graze unconsciously.
- If you want a cupcake, eat a cupcake. But don't eat one just because they are in the breakroom.

If you aren't hungry enough to eat an apple, you aren't really hungry.

- In the beginning of this process, as we are making different choices, our bodies will try to tell us we need more sugar or carbs. Don't follow the impulse without asking yourself if you are **actually** hungry.
- Keep fresh fruits and veggies available, and go for those first. If you are actually hungry, an apple and scoop of peanut butter, or carrots and hummus will sound good. Are you actually hungry? Or are you bored?

Making the most of your meals: Eat Slower

- The idea is to create habits that encourage a good relationship with food. We want to **enjoy** food; in a healthy way.
- Drink 8oz of water (half a bottle) 10 minutes before you eat. It will aide with digestion and help your body recognize when it's "full" faster.
- Set your fork down between bites. Chew your food 15-30 times (depending on texture) before swallowing. Then pick up your fork for the next bite. Slow down. **Savor the flavor.**

Affirmations to Try:

(because we know it's hard to get this started)

- ❖ This too shall pass.
- ❖ It is unnecessary to chase. The things that are meant for me, will come to me.
- ❖ I am capable of change.
- ❖ I have control over my reactions.
- ❖ I am worthy of love and respect.
- ❖ Everyday, I fall a little more in love with myself.
- ❖ I am working to build a life filled with happiness.
- ❖ My body is powerful.
- ❖ I am open to abundance.
- ❖ I appreciate the little things.
- ❖ Courage starts with showing up and letting ourselves be seen.
- ❖ My perspective is unique. It is important and it counts.
- ❖ The cracks are where the light gets in.
- ❖ It's okay that I am scared, I can do it anyway.
- ❖ I am the greatest. I said that even before I knew I was. -M. Ali
- ❖ My vibe attracts my tribe.
- ❖ I am an Emotional Asshole, and I embrace where I'm at.
- ❖ I can handle anything that comes my way.
- ❖ I have grown from my mistakes.
- ❖ I am free to pursue my passions.
- ❖ Happiness is a choice, and today, I choose happiness.
- ❖ There are people who love me.
- ❖ Transformations are happening within me, and within my life.
- ❖ I am solution oriented.
- ❖ Today is going to be a great day.
- ❖ I am curious.
- ❖ Today is a new day, and I am open to new experiences.
- ❖ I have hope for the future.
- ❖ I have everything I need to be the best possible version of myself.

Express Yourself:

My Favorite Affirmations:

_____

_____

_____

_____

Today, I am grateful for:

_____

_____

_____

_____

My friends would say my best qualities are:

_____

_____

_____

#EMOTIONAL*asshole*

This exercise is designed to make you think about YOU. We need to understand our own needs, in order to express them. We need to identify the things that bring us joy, before we can embrace them. Your perception matters. It is important. Now, let's figure out the details.

I would encourage you to answer these questions in a journal. But I know journaling's not for everyone, so I am providing some space below.

The Fun Stuff First:

If you could spend a day doing anything you wanted what would it be? (Imagine a world where you aren't tired or stressed, if you didn't need rest, but had energy and a whole day to yourself.)

_____

_____

_____

_____

If you could spend the day doing anything you wanted, with one other person of your choice, what would you do? (Same perfect-world scenario).

_____

_____

What is something you have always wanted to learn?

_____

_____

What is one thing that *always* makes you smile? (like, that I-can't-help-myself smile)

_____

_____

If you could choose one activity to NEVER do again, what would it be?

_____

_____

Who are the top 3 people you enjoy spending time with? (your kids don't count)

_____

_____

_____

What is something you know you are good at, that you actually enjoy?

_____

Physical Needs:

How much sleep do you need to wake up feeling rested?

_____

_____

What time(s) of day do you sleep best?

_____

_____

What is the environment that is most ideal for sleeping? (think lighting, noise, temperature)

_____

_____

What is your favorite way to relax at home?

_____

_____

What is your favorite outdoor activity?

_____

_____

What activity helps you clear your head/mind?

_____

_____

What types of exercise make your body feel good?

_____

_____

_____

Emotional Needs:

This section requires some real self-reflection. It is not selfish to know what you need. It is not selfish to *ask* for what you need. It is important to know your personal boundaries. It is okay for you to hold your boundaries.

At home, what types of things make you feel like you have a partner?

_____

_____

_____

Letting go of all societal or familial expectations, how do you want to be celebrated on your birthday?

_____

_____

_____

If all your future sexual experiences were limited to only what you have regularly done or expressed interest in – would you be sexually satisfied? What do you want to experience that you haven't yet asked for?

_____

_____

_____

When you are upset, how do you want to be treated? (like, really – you can't say you want time to yourself, if that then makes you feel like no-one cares... what do you *really* need?)

_____

_____

Taking Inventory:

Life happens. We all have outside stressors, obligations and expectations. The trouble is, we tend to lose *ourselves* in the chaos of life. And, somewhere along the way we are taught that taking care of You is selfish.

So, take a few minutes to look back through your answers. Use this information to evaluate where your energy is going.

Are you spending time with the people that add to your life? Are you seeking out those experiences that make you smile? Are you embracing your sexuality?

These things deserve your energy. You deserve to have these things in your life.

How much effort do you invest trying to prevent *someone else* from being annoyed? Do you feel like a nag? These things probably don't deserve as much energy as you give them.

Be intentional with where you put your energy. If the thing requires doing – do it, but you don't need to *invest* yourself in it. Decide how much energy your obligations actually require, draw that line, and release yourself from anything beyond that point.

This part is yours, and only yours, to decide.

You get to build your best life.

Now, Let's Get Started, Shall We?

Made in the USA
Middletown, DE
28 October 2023

41400097R00017